MW01200649

'TIL TOMORROW, TALLAHASSEE

A Bedtime Story of the Garnet and Gold

By Angelo Standriff, Bryce Browning, Cory Anderson, Evan Ernst, Jonathan Bursevich, Kyle Kashuck, and Zack Ernst

'Till Tomorrow, Tallahassee
A Bedtime Story of the Garnet and Gold
© 2021 by Zack Ernst.

Printed in the United States of America.
ISBN-13: 978-1-77-8330-1-7

MBK
PUBLISHING

MBK Publishing
Cocoa Beach, Florida

The sun had fallen,
the starlight shone in,
and the young one's dreaming
was about to begin.

So the child asked for a bedtime story, and for that child, I have just the one.

It's a magical tale that is often told, saying goodnight to the garnet and gold.

In Tallahassee, there stands a school.
The one we all love,
that brick-covered jewel.

4

Goodnight to all the
beautiful brick buildings.
And to the fountains, the trees, and
the big open greens.

5

Goodnight to all the talented teams, the players that achieve all of their dreams.

And goodnight to the coaches that lead the way,

preparing the teams for the next day of play.

Oh, but how could I ever forget?

Those great, big stadiums made out
of brick.

Goodnight to the bands
that march across our lands.

Goodnight to the circus
and all the high flyers.
Swinging so quickly, from wire to wire.

12

Goodnight to the students
who make our school great.

Studying under oak trees
in the Sunshine State.

ECON

Goodnight to that great Florida tribe,
whose unconquered spirit fills us with pride.

Goodnight to the Gators that chomp
and the Tigers that roar.

Goodnight to the Hurricanes.
And may they come no more.

Goodnight to you
and goodnight to me.
'Til tomorrow, Tallahassee.

The Grove Museum

Acknowledgments

To help spread the magic of the garnet and gold, we added illustrations depicting some wonderful people who have come through Tallahassee. Those people include the following:

Page 2: Liz Maryanski (longtime FSU VP) reading to her beloved Charlotte.

Page 6 (clockwise from top left): Leyla Erkan, Brooks Koepka, Carson Pickett, and Olivia Bergau.

Page 7 (clockwise from top left): Leonard Hamilton, Mark Krikorian, Sue Semrau, Andre Walsh, Ngoni Makusha, and Kimberly Williams.

Page 8: (clockwise from top left): Bobby Bowden, Mike Martin, Jimmy Black, Dr. Gregory Simmons, and Buster Posey.

Page 11: Brittany Gummerman, Hailey Murphy, and Daniel Mentzer on tuba; Emily Caron as color guard; Alexandra Puckett and Thomas Larger on horn; Jordan Fraze as drum major; Jillian Tapper twirling fire batons; Samuel Maxwell and Benjamin Lages on bass drum.

Page 12: Anastasia Stichter on the left trapeze.

Page 13 (from left to right): Barry Jenkins, Joe O'Shea, Myron Rolle, and Sara Blakely.

Page 14: Cara Castellana reading on Legacy Walk.

Page 16: Christian Provancha (#13), Marcus Maye (#20), John Curtis (#24), and Sammy Watkins (#2).

Page 17: Sean Taylor (#26) running onto the field.

Page 19: The mission of The Grove Museum is to preserve and interpret the Call-Collins House, its surrounding acreage, and its historical collections, in order to engage the public in dialogue about civil rights and American history. Previously home to several generations of the Call and Collins families, most recently LeRoy and Mary Call Collins.

Page 20: Kevin Fulmer and Josh White - the original Garnet and Gold Guys; Winston E. Scott (FSU alum, retired United States Navy Captain, former NASA astronaut, American Hero).

To living the dream...

~MBK

The storytellers would like to thank David Russell and Fabrice Guerrier for their dedication to supporting this book and for taking a chance on this idea. And a heartfelt thank you to Arthur Lin and Rania M. Tulba, and Madlukman who brought this book to life through their wonderful artwork.

Story by Angelo Standriff, Bryce Browning, Cory Anderson, Evan Ernst, Jonathan Bursevich, Kyle Kashuck and Zack Ernst.

Artwork by Arthur Lin, Rania M. Tulba and Madlukman.
Syllble, Inc (2020)

Printed in the USA
CPSIA information can be obtained
at www.ICGtesting.com
LVHW061922030224
770345LV00061B/50